For my father, Daniel. Your example fuels my life's journey. For my son, Sekani, and black boys everywhere. Your life matters.

—AK

To my father, George, who wasn't always present but who wanted me to know my history; to my mother, Wanda, whose strength to fight for life and a sincere desire to educate showed me the courage to lead by example; and to my son, Isaiah, and all black boys around the world to always dream BIG!

—JR

To my brother Cedric. You are an amazing dad to C.J. and Vada. Nuff luv to you!

—KD

Text © 2022 by Ali Kamanda and Jorge Redmond
Illustrations © 2022 by Ken Daley
Cover and internal design © 2022 by Sourcebooks
Sourcebooks and the colophon are registered trademarks of Sourcebooks.
The full color art was created digitally in Photoshop using a Wacom Cintiq tablet.
Published by Sourcebooks eXplore, an imprint of Sourcebooks Kids
P.O. Box 4410, Naperville, Illinois 60567-4410
(630) 961-3900
sourcebookskids.com
Cataloging-in-Publication Data is on file with the Library of Congress.
Source of Production: Wing King Tong Paper Products Co. Ltd., Shenzhen, Guangdong Province, China
Date of Production: February 2022
Run Number: 5024922
Printed and bound in China.
WKT 10 9 8 7 6 5 4 3 2 1

Dear boy, Black boy, rise up, it's time.
It's a new day and a chance to shine.

Shine like the sun, magnificent and bold.

A new chapter begins,
your story's untold.

A story of courage that starts on this day.
Courage like these men who paved a way.

Dear boy,
    Black boy,
        what do you see?

That's Colin Kaepernick taking a knee.

Stand up,
  go ahead and dare to dream.

Dream big, dear boy, like Martin Luther King.

Realize your power,
    you're blessed with talents

like Elijah McCoy, inventing over fifty patents.

Dear boy,
    Black boy,
        what do you love?

Stories of Emory Malick flying high above.

Let's keep it going,
        tell me how you feel.

Brave like William Goines,
the first Black Navy Seal.

Name me a song you really like to hum.

I like Sam Cooke's *"A Change Is Gonna Come."*

Dear boy,
    Black boy,
        what do you read?

Chinua Achebe's poems,
inspirational indeed.

Show me the style of your favorite dance.

Just like Arthur Mitchell,
look at my stance.

Break boundaries,
dear boy,
shape your own fate.

President Barack Obama became the Head of State.

Dear boy, Black boy, what do you see?
I see many faces that look like me.

Yes, it's true and those faces you see,
they are change-makers of your history.

With joy and love, this is written for you.
Believe in yourself and all you can do.

Dear boy, Black boy, now it's your turn.
Work hard, be proud of all that you earn.

The future is now, it's your time to grow.
Grow to inspire and your bright light will show.

Time for an adventure, may your journey begin.
Take a deep breath and feel your power within.

Dear boy, Black boy, I believe in you so.

Let's start your journey—

ready,

set,

go.

COLIN KAEPERNICK (born November 3, 1987) is a civil rights activist and former football quarterback for the San Francisco 49ers of the National Football League (NFL). As a political activist, he knelt during the national anthem at the start of NFL games in protest of police brutality and racial inequality in the United States.

DR. MARTIN LUTHER KING JR.
(January 15, 1929–April 4, 1968) was a Baptist minister and activist who was awarded five honorary degrees, named Man of the Year by Time magazine in 1963, and was the youngest man to have received the Nobel Peace Prize. He became not only the symbolic leader of Black Americans during the American civil rights movement, but also a world figure.

ELIJAH MCCOY (May 2, 1844–October 10, 1929) was an inventor and engineer who received nearly sixty patents over the course of his life. While the majority of his inventions related to steam engines, he also developed designs for an ironing board, a lawn sprinkler, and other machines.

EMORY CONRAD MALICK
(December 29, 1881–January 23, 1959) was an aviation pioneer from Pennsylvania. He received his pilot's license when he was thirty-one years old, making him not only the first African American pilot, but also possibly the first known Black pilot to earn an international license.

WILLIAM GOINES (born September 10, 1936) is the first African American to become a member of the Navy SEALS. After thirty-two years of service, he retired from the Navy as a Master Chief Petty Officer. He was awarded the Bronze Star, the Navy Commendation Medal, the Meritorious Service Medal, a Combat Action Ribbon, and the Presidential Unit Citation.

SAM COOKE (January 22, 1931–December 11, 1964) was a singer, songwriter, and entrepreneur. He is commonly referred to as the "King of Soul" for his distinctive vocals, notable contributions to the genre, and high significance in popular music.

CHINUA ACHEBE (November 16, 1930–March 21, 2013) was a novelist, poet, professor, and critic, and is often called the father of modern African literature. His first novel, *Things Fall Apart*, considered his masterpiece, is the most widely read African novel in modern literature.

ARTHUR MITCHELL (March 27, 1934–September 19, 2018) was a ballet dancer, choreographer, founder, and director of ballet companies. In 1955, he made his debut as the first African American dancer with the New York City Ballet (NYCB), performing in Western Symphony. In 1969, he founded a training school and the first African American classical ballet company, Dance Theatre of Harlem.

BARACK OBAMA (born August 4, 1961) is a politician and attorney who served as the forty-fourth president of the United States from 2009 to 2017. In 2009, he was awarded the Nobel Peace Prize for his extraordinary efforts to strengthen international diplomacy and cooperation between people. As America's first Black president, he continues to serve as an important role model and community figure.